Little Book Of Positivity

For a Fabulous Teen Girl

Quotes and Inspirations to get you through life's little problems and remind you that you are awesome!

By Katie Smile

© Copyright -Katie Smile 2021 - All rights reserved.

The content contained within this book may not be reproduced, duplicated or transmitted without direct written permission from the author or the publisher.

Under no circumstances will any blame or legal responsibility be held against the publisher, or author, for any damages, reparation, or monetary loss due to the information contained within this book. Either directly or indirectly. You are responsible for your own choices, actions, and results.

Legal Notice:

This book is copyright protected. This book is only for personal use. You cannot amend, distribute, sell, use, quote or paraphrase any part, or the content within this book, without the consent of the author or publisher.

Disclaimer Notice:

Please note the information contained within this document is for educational and entertainment purposes only. All effort has been executed to present accurate, up to date, and reliable, complete information. No warranties of any kind are declared or implied. Readers acknowledge that the author is not engaging in the rendering of legal, financial, medical or professional advice. The content within this book has been derived from various sources. Please consult a licensed professional before attempting any techniques outlined in this book.

By reading this document, the reader agrees that under no circumstances is the author responsible for any losses, direct or indirect, which are incurred as a result of the use of the information contained within this document, including, but not limited to, — errors, omissions, or inaccuracies.

Introduction

Firstly, I would like to start this book by saying you are fabulous and amazing. Yes, you probably heard it many times before or not enough, but I mean it when I say you are!

Now truly feel it and tell it to yourself.

I am amazing. Take a deep breath, hold it for a few seconds and breathe out.

This world is full of many exciting twists and turns, but whichever way it takes you, you have to remember you got this, and you can get past anything. Now that's positive thinking!

Whether it is a gloomy Monday or an exciting Friday, whatever the day or the situation, you can get past it. Because it is you! You are strong, brave, and beautiful and can get through anything you put your mind to.

Now say it with me.

I am brave.
I am strong.
And I am beautiful.

"Your self-worth is determined by you. You don't have to depend on someone telling you who you are."

– Beyonce

"You are more powerful than you know; you are beautiful just as you are."

- Melissa Etheridge

Confidence Boost

Being a teenager is one of the most challenging stages of life. You have no idea what is ahead of you or how to handle yourself in a situation properly. Let alone all the hormones in the air that probably give you daily anxiety.

Situations that don't matter as much appear to be taking over your life. And that's okay! You are a Teenager, and it so happens it's not very fun being one. Adults forget to tell you that part, being a teenager is hard. Your body begins to change, and you get your period. It's another thing to add to what already feels like an awkward phase. But let me tell you a little secret: all the feelings and emotions you are feeling right now will all go away one day. So whether you may not see it right now, you will see it one day, and that's a promise. So, isn't it better to know now than later?

Yes, you are fabulous and amazing!

Put a big smile on your face every morning you get up and believe it will be a beautiful day. Happiness is the secret to success in life. If you want to do well in school exams or college, you need to be happy and positive and, most importantly, believe in yourself!

"Happiness and confidence are the prettiest things you can wear."

-Taylor Swift-

Feeling Different: Being Normal is Boring

You are the next generation to something amazing. Feeling different from everyone else is normal. It does not make you strange, weird, or an outsider. It just makes you a teenage girl. Every girl feels the same way. They are just not likely to talk about it. But believe me when I say you are special!

One day you will be someone highly successful with your own house, family, and job, then you will realize that maybe the bad feeling you had before is entirely overtaken by something positive you did later in your life. For example, helping your friends or family, the positive reward you'll get will completely overtake any bad feeling you had within that moment. Or an argument with your family, once you make up after the argument, the positive feeling will overtake the bad feeling of being upset or angry.

You can choose to be whoever you want to be. Normal is boring. Don't be scared of anything; just hold your head up high and just go forward. You can achieve anything you want as long as you are positive and you believe in yourself!

"If you are always trying to be normal, you'll never know how amazing you can be."

-May Angelou

I love my body; Let's get dressed

Waking up everyday and deciding what to wear is one of the more difficult tasks and most teen girls feel exactly the same way. The clothes in the wardrobe always seem to be old or not pretty or just don't seem to fit right. Let alone your body one minute you love it next minute you don't. Well pretty much every girl in the world will say something they are not happy with; about their clothes or their bodies and why?

Regardless of the clothes you wear or your body shape if you are tall, short, fat or skinny every girl is beautiful. You don't have to fit into the media image of a perfect because that image is false. Every year there is a new trend and there is no point following it as it changes constantly. Be proud of who you are!

Even the celebrities who appear with perfect bodies I can tell you now those women will tell you at least one thing they are not happy with when it comes to their body image.

So why is that when they all seem so perfect? Well it all comes down to how you see yourself. You need to love yourself in order to look and feel beautiful. You are a smart and strong young woman and you need to see that your happiness is the only thing that matters. Every part of your body is a part of what makes you. So don't ever feel the need to change it.

BODY IMAGE

Exercise: Practice saying these sentences to yourself.

I love my body.

My body is perfect.

I don't compare myself to others.

I am grateful to my body.

My body is strong and healthy.

I respect my body.

I am beautiful.

Beauty sleep is the secret to a happy life!

In order to feel and look your best, beauty sleep is super important. It allows you to wake up in a good mood and have a great day.

As a teenager, life is full of excitement, and for some reason, it feels like when you go to bed early, you will miss out on something exciting. But that is not the case. In fact, going to bed on time will help you become smarter, more aware, and achieve more in your life than if you didn't. Having the energy and right attitude, you can be unstoppable! There are successful millionaires for a reason.

You must have a good bedtime routine. Believe it or not, but adults have them too!

Once you establish a good bedtime routine, you will see an improvement in your mood and your attitude. The more you stick to your routine, the more benefits you will see. Your skin will have a healthier glow. You will be able to concentrate more in school, and your grade will increase. It's not called beauty sleep for no reason.

"Happiness consists of getting enough sleep. Just that, nothing more." — Robert A. Heinlein

"If you can dream it, you can do it. "

Walt Disney

Friends make life fun!

Making friends and having friends is the fun part of teenage life! It makes life a lot more interesting. It teaches essential skills that will become useful later in life. So whether you have loads of friends or just a handful, know you are very lucky!

You must look out for your friends and show them the difference between right and wrong even when you are having a great time. Someone always has to be responsible to keep you all safe.

The adventures of friendships and life ahead of you have no limits. Friends come and go. Some friendships may cause heartbreak, but you need to be yourself and never change or do anything that will go against what you know is right and wrong or who you are.

You are amazing, and the right friends will see that too. If they don't, that means you haven't met the right friends yet.

But that's okay! Something exciting to look forward to.

"Be who you are and say what you feel, because those who mind don't matter and those who matter don't mind."

-Dr Suess

No relationship drama until I'm older.

You are a fabulous young lady with your whole life at your feet. Nothing is more exciting than the magic ahead of you, so believe me when I tell you relationships are a distraction and do not add any value to the amazing young woman you are! There's no rush. The more educated and smarter you are, the more control and freedom you will have in the future.

When you are older, you will understand the importance of self success and achievements. It's better to buy yourself something than have someone else buy it for you. This is called independence, and it is something that no money can buy. This is why it's so important to focus on yourself. So use this time to Improve and love yourself so much that you will only have time for your family and friends. Be the best person you can be, learn to respect yourself and others, and the rest will naturally fall into place at the right time.

Learn to Love YOU first!

"Believe in yourself and you can do unbelievable things."

— Unknown

Don't let Social Media ruin your positivity.

Instagram, Facebook, and Snapchat can cause awkward situations that may not always have a positive outcome. To be fabulous and safe, you should maintain a distance from rude conversations and always be cautious. Any comments that make you feel uncomfortable, you should always tell an adult. This is very important as there are many bad people online that could lie to you, so never give your information to anyone. Avoid chat rooms as no adults are supervising them and anyone can speak to you.

Using an online platform such as Instagram can negatively affect your life if you're not careful. Many influencers have false images of themselves that have been photoshopped, which is not what they look like in real life. They are not that skinny or have flawless skin. Everyone is human at the end of the day, and no one is perfect. They have fat on their body and spots; they just hide it from you. So always remember you are fabulous and unique.

Never compare yourself to anyone, especially with celebrities!

"Be proud to be Original and not a copy of someone else" -Kamile. V

"No matter what you look like or think you look like, you're special, and loved, and perfect just the way you are." -

-Ariel Winter

Practice Self Love

Exercise: Repeat it to yourself:

I love myself.

I accept myself.

I am worthy.

I deserve to be happy.

I don't need to be perfect.

I don't need to be perfect to make people like me

I accept my flaws.

I love and accept myself

I forgive myself for my mistakes.

I think positive thoughts about myself.

I speak to myself with kindness.

It's okay to be sad.

It's okay to be angry.

It's okay to be scared.

Arguments are not worth it!

As much as the anger and all the emotions seem relevant at that point in time, it really is just a waste of your energy and time that you can't get back, especially when you are a teenager. It affects your mood and your positivity and others around you. The people you care about get upset, and some words are hard to take back. So it's really worth asking yourself whether the argument you were having was worth arguing in the first place?

If the argument is settled and a positive outcome is learned, then the argument was worth the fight. You become a better person when you are able to show remorse. It takes a big person to say they are sorry first. Always remember that. If you can be the first to say sorry, especially when you know you were in the wrong, you will gain a massive amount of respect and trust from the people around you. It will also help you develop very useful social skills and confidence that will make you unstoppable when you become a full-grown woman!

Even though an argument is never a good way to put your point across, it is also important for your feelings to be heard, just in the right way. As a teenage girl, you are full of emotions, and sometimes that can be misunderstood. So every time you get angry, try to take a deep breath and talk calmly, and I guarantee you will get a more positive response. It is really easy to confuse the anger and take it out on the wrong person, and usually, it's your family that suffers the most.

POSITIVE COMMUNICATION

Exercise: Practice saying these sentences to yourself

I stand up for myself

I stand up for others.

I speak with kindness

I speak with respect

I respect others

My voice matters.

My opinions matter.

My words have power.

I am responsible for every word I speak.

When others share their feelings and opinions, I listen.

Don't let anyone one steal your shine!

As you go through life, you might find a few people who might be jealous of you and would want to take your shine away from you. Always remember, whatever the situation, there is only one of you in the whole universe, and that cannot be replaced or copied. So regardless of the jealousy of others, you must carry on and be yourself.

Keep the negativity out of your life, especially when it comes to close friends, and their opinions, as that could really affect your thinking and decision making. Always trust your gut. If it takes losing a close friend, just remember some people leave your life for a reason; usually, it's to make it better or open up new doors to bigger things. So as much as it may seem painful at the time, you should always look for the positive side as it always gets better sooner or later in time.

Protecting yourself from negative people allows you to think bright into the future and have a clear direction to what you want in life.

"The woman who does not require validation from anyone is the most feared individual on the planet."

-Mohadesa Najumi

Bullying is not cool

Many teenage girls experience bullying regularly, and it's unacceptable. It creates a feeling of loneliness and rejection. It takes away every good part of you and makes you shy away as a person, and that's never okay and should not be ignored. It's actually the bullies that have the most significant problems hence why they bully in the first place. They want to take away your positivity and make you feel like they do for a second, to bring you down to their level. You must not let them and report the bullies straight away. Whether it's to family or a school teacher, you need to stop it from happening and get them the help they need.

Bullying can take many forms, whether it's online at school or college face to face, and many other examples don't let anyone affect your Happiness or change you. You are awesome and don't need that negativity in your life.

SELF-ESTEEM AND CONFIDENCE

Exercise: Practice saying these sentences to yourself

I am awesome!

I am brave.

I am strong.

I am confident.

I believe in myself.

I feel proud of myself.

I am important.

I trust myself.

I listen to my heart.

"Surround yourself with those who believe in you. Your life is too important for anything less"

-Steve Goodier

Focus on the positive and not the negative

Whether it's friendships, school, family life, or just teen life situations, there will be many excuses to feel sorry for yourself and focus on the negative. However, if you only focus on the negative and act on it, you will get bad results. For example, if you have an exam coming up and you are struggling but feel there is no point in trying, you will get a bad result. However, if you look at it in a positive way, even though you may be struggling on the topic, if you get extra help and try hard, you will pass your exam and get a good grade.

In order to be successful in anything you do, you must have the right attitude. If you have the right attitude and you are a positive person to be around, you will gain lots of rewards, such as big friendship groups, successful education, and great family life. This is because rather than moping around and not getting anything done, you are being strong and taking control of your life. Once you accomplish your goal whether it's amazing grades or a fantastic job, and you will see everything you were going through that seemed so stressful was actually just a small part of your journey.

Always aim for the stars regardless of the ups or down!

Life always gets better!

"Everything will be okay in the end.

If it's not okay, it's not the end. "

-John Lennon

If you feel a little overwhelmed here are few tips to help you :

1. Take a break and hydrate. Dehydration can negatively affect your mood, and we don't want that do we?

2. Make few playlists of different styles of music. You will sometimes find listening to a different genre can change your mood and sprinkle some much needed positivity for the mind and soul.

3. Check yourself: if you feel you find yourself saying 'i can't do this or 'it's too much, that means you need to take a pause. This is where your support system comes in. It's a lot easier doing something together with some help from a friend or relative than having to do everything by yourself, including when you are feeling anxious and overwhelmed.

4. Move yourself to a more positive environment. If you find the people around you are affecting your mood negatively or making you feel uncomfortable, just remove yourself from the situation. You will find that quite often in life there are some people who just take up all your energy and time and consume your life. This is where, as mentioned previously; you need to set boundaries. It's okay to say NO and remove yourself from the negativity.

5. Most importantly, take a breather. Learn to take some time for yourself and get all your thoughts together, whether it's excusing yourself to go to the toilet and have some privacy there or going outside for a few minutes just to be alone with you. This time is crucial as it allows you to listen to yourself, your needs, and what would make you happy? You then pull yourself and carry on!

Regardless of what techniques you use for self-care, it is important to prioritize yourself. Your well-being always comes first. In order to help someone else, you sometimes need to help yourself first. It is only through a healthy state of mind that you can reach your full potential and succeed in life. There are no limits. As long as you are looking after yourself, eating well, exercising, and most importantly, maintaining your happiness, you will glide through life and its stressors.

In Conclusion

Life will take you through many ups and downs, a bit like a rollercoaster, and it's up to you how you are willing to deal with it. You can get up in the morning and say to yourself, I'm going to have a fantastic day with all your friends and do well in your studies, or you can get up in the morning and think life is horrible and fail, which one do you think will make you most successful? Yes, the positive way! If you practice the exercises in this book it will allow you to achieve a positive outlook on yourself and others around.

To maintain a positive lifestyle, you must also make sure you are also eating a healthy diet full of fruit and veg and getting a good night's rest with a healthy routine.

If you have positively enjoyed this book please leave a review on amazon!

"Sometimes the best goal you can set is just to get out of bed every day. If you can succeed at this, then other things become possible."

~-Cynthia Patterson

"The future belongs to those who believe in the beauty of their dreams"

Eleanor Roosevelt

Resources

Fenner, P. (2020, May 14). *20 Inspiring Quotes for Your Teenager*. Breakthrough Homeschooling. https://breakthroughhomeschooling.com/20-inspiring-quotes-for-teens/

Burnett, H. (2020, June 2). *18 Inspirational Quotes Every Mom Needs To Share (If She Wants To Raise A Fearless Girl)*. Word To Your Mother. https://wordtoyourmotherblog.com/inspirational-quotes-by-famous-women/

Lagacé, M. (2021, January 18). *120 Inspirational Quotes For Teens (For A Meaningful Life)*. Wisdom Quotes. https://wisdomquotes.com/inspirational-quotes-for-teens/

Lagudu, S. (2018a, December 18). *51 Inspirational Quotes On Teenagers' Life.* MomJunction. https://www.momjunction.com/articles/teen-life-quotes_00462262/

Calm, S. C. (2018, September 7). *50 of the Best Sleep Quotes.* SensaCalm. https://www.sensacalm.com/blogs/news/best-sleep-quotes

Motivational Quotes. (n.d.). BrainyQuote. Retrieved February 22, 2021, from https://www.brainyquote.com/topics/motivational-quotes

Mentlik, C. (2020, December 8). *108 Positive Affirmations to Empower Tweens.* Inner Rainbow Project. https://www.innerrainbowproject.com/108-positive-affirmations-empower-girls/

www.ingramcontent.com/pod-product-compliance
Lightning Source LLC
Chambersburg PA
CBHW030917080526
44589CB00010B/341